Hinduism:

Signs, Symbols, and Stories

Cath Senker

PowerKiDS
press.

New York

Published in 2010 by The Rosen Publishing Group Inc.
29 East 21st Street, New York, NY 10010

First Edition

Library of Congress Cataloging-in-Publication Data

Senker, Cath.
  Hinduism: signs, symbols, stories / Cath Senker.
      p. cm. -- (Religious signs, symbols, and stories)
  Includes index.
  ISBN 978-1-4358-3038-7 (library binding)
  ISBN 978-1-4358-3046-2 (paperback)
  ISBN 978-1-4358-3054-7 (6-pack)
  1. Hinduism--Juvenile literature. 1. Title.
  BL1203.S46 2010
  294.5--dc22
                                            2008051896

Manufactured in China

Disclaimer
Although every effort has been made to offer accurate and clearly expressed information, the author and publisher acknowledge that some explanations may not be relevant to those who practice their faith in a different way.

Acknowledgements
The author and publisher would like to thank the following for their pictures to be reproduced in this publication: Cover Illustrations: Roberto Tomei (both); Ajay Verma/Corbis: 28; ArkReligion.com/Helene Rogers: 7, 16, 20; Arvind Garg/Corbis: 17; Blaine Harrington III/Corbis: 8; Chris Fairclough: 9, 12 (both), 18, 21; Claire Stout/World Religions Photo Library/Alamy: 24; David R. Frazier Photolibrary Inc/Alamy: 27; Eddie Gerald/Alamy: 25; Kamal Kishore/Reuters/Corbis: 26; Mike Abrahams/Alamy: 14.

The author would like to thank the following for permission to reproduce material in this book: p.5 the sun god Surya from 'Ra, Surya, Rangi, Atea—Myths of Sun God' by Sunil Deepak, http://www.kalpana.it/eng/writer/sunil_deepak/sun_myths.htm; p.9 'Namaste' from Ottawa Mindfulness, http://ottawamindfulness.ca/Newsletter/Archives/1999/September/Namaste/tabid/299/Default.aspx; p.11 translation of the Gayatri-mantra from http://www.indiaparenting.com/ rhymes/prayers/001.shtml; p.15 recipe adapted from http://www.girlsinc.org/gc/inc/Kheer.htm and http://foodsofindia.blogspot.com/2005/08/recipe-kheer.html; p.19 recipe for Simply Wonderfuls from http://www.harekrsna.com/practice/prasadam/seva/handouts.htm; p.21 translation of Jaya Jagadeesha Hare (Temple Prayer) from http://www.hindutemplede.com/aratiPrayers.shtml#java and http://sanskaraastha.blogspot.com/2007/09/temple-prayer-aarti-om-jaya-jagadheesha.html.

With special thanks to Alka Vekaria.

The author and publisher would like to thank the following models: Celine Clark, Isobel Grace, Hari Johal, and Charlie Pengelly.

Note to parents and teachers: The projects in this book are designed to be made by children. However, we do recommend adult supervision at all times since the Publisher cannot be held responsible for any injury caused while undertaking any activities.

Contents

Activities

There are lots of activities throughout
this book.

You can **read** traditional
tales, stories from holy
books, folk tales, poems, and prayers
on pages 5, 9, 11, 13, 17, 23, 25, 27.

You can **sing** songs and
chant on pages 7, 21.

You can **make** traditional
food on pages 15, 19.

You can **make** art patterns
on page 29.

Signs and symbols

A sign usually has one clear meaning. You have probably seen emergency exit signs over doors at school. The sign means "if there is danger, leave through here."

The swastika is a Hindu symbol.

Symbols can have different meanings. For example, the **swastika** is an ancient Hindu symbol for good luck. It points in all directions to show that the **Supreme Being**, **Brahman**, is everywhere. The Nazis, who ruled Germany from 1933 to 1945, took

up the swastika. They changed its meaning and used it as a symbol for the victory of the Nazi German people over others.

The swastika and the sun god

From ancient times, the Hindu swastika stood for the sun god, Surya. This story is about how our **solar system** came about.

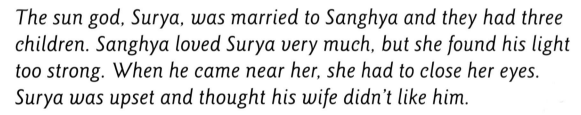

The sun god, Surya, was married to Sanghya and they had three children. Sanghya loved Surya very much, but she found his light too strong. When he came near her, she had to close her eyes. Surya was upset and thought his wife didn't like him.

*One day, Sanghya left home, leaving in her place a **double** called Chaaya. At first Surya didn't notice. When he realized Chaaya was not his wife, he searched for Sanghya. He found her in the form of a horse. She was praying. He turned into a horse and went up to her.*

Sanghya explained that Surya's light was too strong for her, so Surya divided his light into 16 parts. He created the earth and all the planets from 15 of the parts and kept just one-sixteenth of the light for himself.

The aum symbol

The **aum** symbol is **sacred**. Aum stands for Brahman, the Supreme Being. The Aum symbol represents the sound of Brahman, or God. It is a sound as well as a symbol. Hindus believe that the creation of the universe began with the sound of aum. They chant aum as a **mantra** (prayer), a sacred sound with spiritual powers. It is the most important Hindu mantra.

This is the aum symbol.

Aum is made up of three sounds: a, u, and m. The sounds stand for waking, dreaming, and deep sleep. Together, they stand for a person's spiritual side.

Chanting aum

Everyone in the group should sit or stand in a circle. Close your eyes and focus on your breathing. Take a few slow breaths. Notice the air flowing in and out of your body. Then begin to chant "aum." You can all chant the sound when you are ready. There is no need to begin and end at the same time. Continue for a few minutes. After you stop, take a few more deep breaths before you open your eyes.

Talk with others about how it felt while you were chanting.

Namaste

Hindus believe in a Supreme Being named Brahman. Some Hindus call Brahman "God." Brahman is everywhere but cannot be seen.

For many Hindus, Brahman has no shape. Brahman is in all of us. When Hindus greet each other or say goodbye, they put their hands together in the prayer position and bow their head slightly. They say "**namaste**" (said like this: "namastay"). It means "respect to God within you." This shows respect to God and to the **soul** of the person—the real self, which is made up mostly of the mind.

Hindus greet each other with namaste.

Namaste

*I **honor** the place in you
in which the entire
universe dwells.
I honor the place in you
which is of love, of truth,
of light, and of peace.
When you are in
that place in you,
and I am in
that place in me,
We are One.*

Deities

Hindus worship many different **deities**. The deities symbolize the different forms of Brahman. The three main deities are Brahma the creator, Vishnu the protector, and Shiva the destroyer of the universe.

Shiva is in the form of a dancer named Nataraja, who destroys the universe and recreates it again.

Murtis, or sacred images, are symbols of the deities. Hindus believe that Brahman is present in the murtis. Through them, Brahman accepts the worshipers' love. The murtis help the worshipers to focus their minds on Brahman.

Mantras to the gods

The goddess, Shakti, is a main deity. She stands for Mother Nature. Shakti has different forms. As Parvati, she is kind and generous. As Durga, she is warlike, to protect the people who worship her.

The Gayatri-mantra is a mantra to Gayatri, the sun goddess. In **Sanskrit**, the Hindu holy language, the mantra starts with aum, meaning "O God." It has several translations —let's read one.

O God, you are the giver of life
[Oh God, you give life]

remover of pain and sorrow
[you take away pain and sorrow]

the bestower of happiness
[you give happiness]

may your light destroy our sins
[may your light destroy the bad things we do]

and may you illumine our intellect to lead us along the righteous path.
[light up our minds so that we live in the right way.]

Ganesh

Hindus worship different deities. There are many popular deities, including Rama and Sita (see pages 22–23) and Ganesh.

Hindus believe that Ganesh removes obstacles—problems and things that are in the way. He helps people with new projects. Hindus worship Ganesh when they are about to start anything new, such as moving to a new house or going on a trip.

Ganesh has an elephant's head. His big head stands for wisdom and understanding. His four arms show that God is everywhere. He has a huge pot belly, so he can take on the sorrows of the universe.

This is a murti of Ganesh.

This is a murti of Hanuman (see page 23).

Let's read a folk tale

How Ganesh got his head

Ganesh's mother was the goddess Parvati and his father the god, Shiva. He didn't always have the head of an elephant.

Ganesh's father went away for many years. When Shiva returned, Ganesh did not recognize the stranger with matted hair and snakes wriggling around him. He would not let his father into the house.

Shiva was angry with the boy standing in his way, and he cut off his head with one swipe of his sword. When Parvati came out, she cried, "You have killed our son!" Shiva felt terrible. He promised he would replace their son's head with the head of the first animal he could find. Shiva searched far and wide, until finally he spotted a baby elephant. He chopped off the elephant's head, rushed home, and attached it to Ganesh's body.

The holy cow

Most Hindus are **vegetarian**. They believe that all living things have souls, so it is wrong to eat animals.

Foods made from milk are very important to Hindus. At the festival of **Diwali**, for example, they enjoy kheer, a sweet, milky pudding.

In India, cows are allowed to wander freely in the streets.

As a giver of milk, the cow is holy to Hindus. The cow is a symbol of how the earth provides us with food. Even Hindus who eat some meat will never eat any meat from the cow.

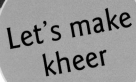

Let's make
kheer

Recipe for kheer, a Diwali recipe

Ask an adult to help you cook

You will need:

1/2 cup basmati rice
4 cups milk
1/4 cup raisins
I cup sugar
I teaspoon cardamom or nutmeg
1/4 cup shredded almonds or cashew nuts
A few strands of saffron (if you like)

1. *Boil the rice in the milk on medium heat until it is cooked. Stir regularly.*

2. *Add the sugar and stir well.*

3. *Take off the heat and add the other ingredients. Stir.*

4. *Serve warm or cold.*

Preparing for worship

As well as performing prayers at home, Hindus also make **puja** (worship) in the **mandir**, their place of worship. A mandir is Brahman's home on earth.

At the mandir, a **priest** takes care of the deities. If they are not looked after, it is believed they will leave.

When worshipers arrive, they take off their shoes as a symbol of respect for the mandir and to keep it clean. When they enter the mandir, they ring a bell.

The ringing of the bell is a symbol of waking up the deities, so that they know the worshipers have arrived.

Prayer

A sloka is a verse to praise God. It is offered to the deities.

In Sanskrit:

Gurubra rhmaa gururvishhnuh gururdevo maheshvarah guruH saakshaatparabrahma tasmai shrii guravenamah

In English:

I bow to that Shri Guru, who embodies [brings together] the presence of Brahma, Vishnu the supreme, and Shiva.

(Shri is a term of respect. The Guru is the Master or God.)

Making offerings

The murtis stand on the **shrine**. Viewing the deities on the shrine is special to Hindus. It is called **darshan**.

Fruit and flowers are given to offer thanks to the deities. Flowers stand for offering the heart to God.

During puja, worshipers make **offerings** of flowers and food to the murtis. At the end of worship, they receive **prashad**. It is usually fruit, nuts, or sweets.

Prashad is a symbol of the giving and receiving between worshipers and God. After the offerings are made to the deities, they become holy. The priest returns part of the deities to the worshipers to bring God's **blessings** upon them.

Recipe for Simply Wonderfuls

Ask an adult to help you cook

These sweets are sometimes used as prashad.

You will need:

2 cups powdered milk
1 cup unsalted butter
1 3/4 cups confectioners' sugar
1/2 cup raisins or chopped nuts

1. Melt the butter in a small-sized pan.

2. Remove from the heat and cool slightly.

3. Add the confectioners' sugar and stir until it melts.

4. Add the powdered milk slowly and mix it in.

5. Now squeeze a small amount of the mixture into a ball. If it is too wet, add some powdered milk. If it is too dry, add some more melted butter.

6. Roll the mixture into balls about I inch (2 1/2 cm) across.

The arti ceremony

The **arti** ceremony uses fire.
It is an important part of puja.

The arti tray

- The five arti lamps stand
  for the five elements
  people need to survive:
  water, fire, earth, air, and
  space. They also symbolize
  the five human senses.
  People use all of their
  senses during worship.
- Worshipers light the lamps to show they
  want to move from darkness to light.
  God brings them knowledge.
- Flowers symbolize the opening of the
  heart during the ceremony. They are
  also a symbol of beauty.
- Water is a symbol of being pure.

The arti tray is moved in a circle in front of the deities to honor them. In return, the worshipers receive blessings from the fire. They pass their fingers over the flame and then touch their forehead.

Let's sing a song

Arti song

This song is often sung during arti. Here is part of it, in English:

Jaya Jagadeesha Hare (Temple Prayer)

Glory to the Lord Of The Universe
Who removes in a moment
The troubles of devotees [people who worship the Lord]
And the sufferings of the poor

One who meditates [thinks deeply] on you is blessed
Sorrow is removed from mind and heart
Happiness and wealth come to the home
Pain is wiped away from the body

You are my mother and father
In whom else can I take refuge [shelter]
No other than you do I accept
Of whom I accept everything

You are the complete being, the Supreme Self
You are the knower of all hearts
You are Brahman, the infinite Lord [Lord without limits]
You are the Lord of all.

Stories and tales

The Hindu holy books contain many stories about the deities and they are full of symbols.

The *Ramayana* is one of the most popular tales. The main characters are Rama and Sita, who have many adventures.

*In the **Ramayana**, Sita is captured by Ravana and taken away from Rama. Ravana symbolizes evil in the story.*

They stand for the ideal married couple, who love each other through both the good and the terrible times. They are symbols of the Hindu ideal of **dharma**— the right way of living. The Ramayana also symbolizes the battle between good and evil.

The *Ramayana*: Rama and Sita

A king in ancient times had four sons by three different wives. The eldest was Rama. When Rama married the princess Sita, the king decided it was time to give up his throne to him.

However, his newest wife was jealous. She wanted her own son to be king. Many years before, she had saved the king's life and he had promised her two wishes. Now she wanted to have one of her wishes. She wished for Rama to be sent away for 14 years, so that her son could rule the kingdom.

*Rama and Sita disappeared into the forest, thinking that at least they could stay together. But then the wicked **demon** king, Ravana, stole Sita away. Rama spent long years searching for her. In the end, good won over evil. Rama eventually found Sita with the help of the monkey king, Hanuman. The 14 years were over, and the couple returned home to great celebrations.*

Cycle of life

Hindus believe that all living things go through a cycle of birth, death, and rebirth. After death, the soul passes from one life to the next. Hindus carry out special ceremonies, called rites of passage, to help people along the journey.

Whether you are **reborn** to a good or a bad life depends on your **karma**—your actions, good or bad, in this life.

Cutting a boy's hair for the first time is a rite of passage in the Hindu faith.

Hindu rites of passage symbolize this belief. For example, a baby boy has his first haircut when he is about a year old. Hindus believe that cutting the hair removes the karma of the child's previous life, so he can start a new one.

A shikha for safety

*The ancient Indian surgeon, Sushruta, believed that it was important to leave a tuft of hair uncut at the haircutting ceremony. This was the **shikha**. A large shikha was left to grow thick and strong, while the rest of the head remained smooth and bald.*

The shikha covered the crown of the head and a large part of the brain. Sushruta believed that this part of the head was delicate, and a blow to the crown would cause death. Also, the shikha protected it from the heat of the sun.

Holi

Holi is a spring festival. People light bonfires, join processions, sing and dance, and enjoy water fights. Holi symbolizes two stories.

At Holi, people remember Krishna, who loved to play tricks. He used to throw colored water over the milkmaids. Everyone goes out into the streets for a big water fight—young and old, men and women alike.

People throw colored water over each other when they celebrate Holi.

The bonfires are a symbol of the story of Prahlad and Holika. They stand for the burning away of greed and evil spirits, and the victory of good over evil.

Prahlad and Holika

King Hiranyakashipu was a powerful and greedy king. He wanted everyone in his kingdom to worship him instead of God. Yet his son Prahlad refused, and continued to worship the Lord Vishnu.

King Hiranyakashipu was angry. He was prepared to murder his own son if he would not do as he was told. The king asked his wicked sister, Holika, to help him set a trap for Prahlad. Holika had a special power that meant she did not get burned by fire. She tricked Prahlad into sitting on her lap, and then a huge bonfire was lit beneath them. Terrified, Prahlad expected to be burned to death.

Yet, because she was using her power for evil, Holika's plan failed. Instead of Prahlad, it was she who was burned to ashes in the flames. The young man walked away unharmed.

Diwali

In the *Ramayana* story, Rama and Sita returned home on the night of the new moon. It was completely dark. Hindus celebrate their return at Diwali, in October or November. They light oil lamps to remember how candles guided Rama and Sita home. The lamps are also a symbol of light overcoming darkness—that is, good winning over evil.

Diwali also symbolizes a fresh start. People spring clean the mandir and their home. They light lamps to welcome Lakshmi, the goddess of wealth. They hope for a good year ahead.

To encourage Lakshmi to enter their homes and the mandir, people make bright **rangoli** patterns at the door.

People light oil lamps in patterns for Diwali.

Make rangoli patterns

Rangoli patterns use shapes.
You can use circles, squares,
or rectangles, or all three.
The patterns are often
symmetrical and
show things from
nature. Try simple flower
or star shapes, or make
animals or plants. People
make rangoli patterns with
their fingers using flour, grains
of rice, or colored chalk.

You will need:

Paper plates
A pen
Glue
Selection of lentils and beans

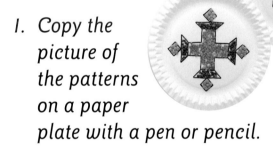

1. Copy the
   picture of
   the patterns
   on a paper
   plate with a pen or pencil.

2. You can color in the
   patterns or stick lentils
   and beans down with glue.

3. Remember to keep the raw
   lentils and beans away
   from your mouth. Wash
   your hands well after
   this activity.

arti Lighting candles and moving them in a circle in front of images of deities to honor them.

aum A symbol and sound that stands for Brahman, the Supreme Being.

blessings God's help and protection.

Brahman The Supreme Being, who some Hindus call "God."

darshan When worshipers visit the mandir for a sight of the deities.

deities Forms of God.

demon Being that behaved badly in previous lives and does bad things in this life.

dharma Living in the right way.

Diwali The festival of lights celebrated by Hindus.

double A person who looks exactly like another.

honor To show great respect.

karma The belief that your actions in this life affect your future in this life and the next.

mandir The Hindu place of worship.

mantra A sacred word or prayer that is said again and again.

murtis Images of a deity, used in worship.

namaste The Hindu greeting, which means "respect to God within you."

offerings Things that are offered to the deities on the shrine.

prashad Food that is offered to the deities and then shared after worship.

priest A person who performs religious duties in the mandir.

puja Worship at home or in the mandir.

rangoli A beautiful pattern made at the entrance to homes and mandirs to welcome deities and visitors.

reborn Born again.

sacred Holy—connected with God.

Sanskrit The Hindu holy language, which is used during worship.

shikha The tuft of hair left uncut when a baby boy has his first haircut.

shrine A place where the murtis stand.

solar system The sun and all the planets that move around it.

soul A person's real self, which is made up mostly of the mind.

Supreme Being The Hindu idea of God. The Supreme Being has no form and is everywhere. Yet, images standing for the different aspects of God are used to help people worship.

swastika An ancient Hindu symbol that stands for good luck.

symmetrical With two halves the same size and shape.

vegetarian A person who eats no meat or fish.

Books to read

Let's Find Out About: Hindu Mandirs
by Anita Ganeri (Raintree, 2005)

Hindu Prayer and Worship
by Rasamandala Das and Anita Ganeri
(Sea to Sea Publications, 2008)

The Ramayana and Hinduism
by Anita Ganeri (Smart Apple Media, 2003)

Traditional Religious Tales: Hindu Stories
by Anita Ganeri (Picture Window Books, 2006)

Where We Worship: Hindu Mandir
by Angela Wood (Gareth Stevens
Publishing, 2000)

Web Sites

Due to the changing nature of Internet links, PowerKids Press has developed an online list of Web sites related to the subject of this book. This site is updated regularly. Please use this link to access this list:
www.powerkidslinks.com/sss/hindu

𑁍 Index